THE TROUBLE WITH LIGHT

Miller Williams Poetry Series
EDITED BY PATRICIA SMITH

THE TROUBLE WITH LIGHT

JEREMY MICHAEL CLARK

The University of Arkansas Press | Fayetteville | 2024

ISBN: 978-1-68226-249-8
eISBN: 978-1-61075-818-5

28 27 26 25 24   5 4 3 2 1

Manufactured in the United States of America

∞ The paper used in this publication meets the minimum requirements of the American National Standard for Permanence of Paper for Printed Library Materials Z39.48-1984.

Library of Congress Cataloging-in-Publication Data

Names: Clark, Jeremy Michael, 1990– author.
Title: The trouble with light / Jeremy Michael Clark.
Description: Fayetteville : The University of Arkansas Press, 2024. |
  Series: Miller Williams poetry series | Summary: "In 'The Trouble with
  Light,' Jeremy Michael Clark reflects on the legacy of familial trauma
  as he delves into questions about belonging, survival, knowledge, and
  self-discovery in unflinching lyrical poems. Largely set in the poet's
  hometown of Louisville, Kentucky, Clark's portraits of interiority
  gracefully juxtapose the sorrows of alienation and self-neglect with the
  restorative power of human connection"— Provided by publisher.
Identifiers: LCCN 2023043801 (print) | LCCN 2023043802 (ebook) |
  ISBN 9781682262498 (paperback) | ISBN 9781610758185 (ebook)
Subjects: LCGFT: Poetry.
Classification: LCC PS3603.L36463 T76 2024 (print) | LCC PS3603.L36463
  (ebook) | DDC 811/.6—dc23/eng/20230927
LC record available at https://lccn.loc.gov/2023043801
LC ebook record available at https://lccn.loc.gov/2023043802

Supported by the Miller and Lucinda Williams Poetry Fund

How dumb he was to wipe the blood from his eye.

—Gerald Stern

CONTENTS

SERIES EDITOR'S PREFACE

The world has long flirted with implosion, and implosion has finally taken notice.

As I write this, we flail in a stubborn, insistent—and increasingly deadly—tangle of cultural, political, and global devastation. We once again speak of war as a given, a necessary and common occurrence. We're pummeled with unfiltered images of everything hatred can do, its snarl and grimace and spewed invectives, its stone in the pit of the belly. The air we breathe is no longer willing to nurture us, the earth no longer willing to be our unquestioning home. It's becoming increasingly difficult to find a direction that harbors solace or shelter.

And in the midst of our emotional desolation, we've been told— once again, dammit—that poetry is dead. It seems to die biannually, right on some crackpot schedule, its death often coinciding with the death of flared jeans, boy bands, and diet soda.

And once again—fresh from a deep dive into poetry that jolts, rearranges, rollicks, rebirths, convinces, destructs, and rebuilds—I am moved to dissent.

Poetry, at least the way it reaches me, has never been remotely close to quietus. It may occasionally be cloaked in a pensive or embarrassed silence or tangled in an overwrought and overwhelming barrage of language. It may be overly obsessed with sparing the delicate feelings of *someone* or maintaining the tenuous status of *something*. It can be tiring or inappropriate, or flat and studious, or heartless, or saddled with too *much* heart. Its pulse is sometimes so faint that its bare-there is often mistaken for that long-predicted demise.

At the biannual funeral, there is misguided celebration by tweed-swaddled critics, wheezing academics, and those who've spent their lives perplexed by poetry's omnipresent sway. It's a limit affair that makes them all feel better. But there's no weep or caterwaul, because actual poets—and gleeful lovers of sonnet, caesura, and stanza—have no reason whatsoever to grieve.

In fact, I come to you with reasons for rejoice, reasons to believe that poetry is not only alive, but that it is electric and naughtily raucous.

I must thank my tenacious and thoughtful readers, who consistently pass along the work that surprises, intrigues, and changes me. My readers are poets I revere—they are like me and unlike me, and the one thing they have in common is the consistency of their work. I've been contacted by people who say that the standard I've set for selection is virtually impossible.

I'm about to introduce you to four poets who seem, somehow, to have done the impossible.

Of course, picking a "winner" makes absolutely no sense in this context. Depending on the day and time I sat down to consider the finalists, their positions changed. The competition was just that heated. I want all of them to know, right now, that *any of you could have won*.

And all of them deserved to win.

Let's look at our—for lack of a better term—"runner-ups."

Adele Elise Williams's *Wager* was undoubtedly crafted to upend the familiar—both narratively and sonically—and turn it into something unflinchingly fresh. Language, as some of us know, exists to be fiddled with, and Williams, a storyteller who steadfastly refuses lyrical compliance, has a grand ol' time reintroducing us to what we assume we already know. I love a poet who runs rampant, rebelling against restraint—however, that by no means indicates a lack of discipline or a desire to cloak the work in "device." These poems hit home because they pull us into the poet's rampaging narrative, because we are all creatures of story who crave POVs that rouse us and redefine what we see. As a former "performance poet" (whatever that means these days), I took particular joy in reading *Wager* aloud—more than once, more than twice—and reveling in what Williams's deftly crafted ditties do to the air.

I mean, this is the opening of "Gal," the *first poem in the book*:

> She's so helpless and the undertone
> is spooky-ooky! She's so natural

and the assumption is heaven high
is gilded and gyrific, is like chakras.
I mean, placement for purpose. I mean,
outward burst. She's so blond!

And if that aural deliciousness puts you in the mood for play—
not so fast. These poems swirl with shadow when you least expect
it. The next time poetry dies, I highly suggest a massive infusion
of—this.

Self-Mythology, by Chinese-Iranian poet Saba Keramati, is the
book we need right now, as so many of us explore our hyphenated
selves, searching for meaning in being not all one and not all the
other, wondering if and where we are truly rooted.

But even as we turn inward for clues, we're a suspicious, judg-
mental lot, and so much of the volatile confusion that marks our days
springs from a brash selfishness—our unwillingness to consider the
person next to us, to learn what that person feels and believes, the
tenets they live by. Keramati first confronts the formidable task of
knowing the body and mind she inhabits—her backdrops and loom-
ing future, her vulnerabilities and failures, her reactions to loss and
love, the experience of being two in the body of one. In her poem
"The Act," she writes, "I'll always be / here, chameleoning myself //
with every shift of the light."

So many writers are telling these stories—or making their best
attempts to. Keramati avoids the many pitfalls of addressing a com-
plex identity—you won't find confounding DIY tanglings of language
or an unwavering eye fixed on the myriad metaphors of culture
clash. *Self-Mythology*'s poems unreel with revelation, undaunted soul-
searching, and crisp, deliberate lyric:

Let me write myself here, with these symbols
I claim to know, swear are in my lineage—

proving myself to my own desire
to be seen.

To be seen. To be heard. To grieve and rejoice and question out loud. All while so many demand a Black silence.

It has been decided, obviously by those who decide such things, that Black folks have made entirely too much noise about inconsequential things like—well, history. Our collective history, and the history of each one of us, the past that won't stop quivering in our chests. All those histories hastily being rescripted. Refocused. Disappeared.

In the midst of a country's fervent undertaking to render the Black voice inconsequential to both that country's backdrop and its future, Jeremy Michael Clark's insistence upon light—troubled though it may be—is imperative and rebelliously wrought. The huge story rests within the smaller one. Clark chronicles the fevered intersections of love and fear, and whole restless worlds reside in each line. Truths are unrelenting here—plain truths that agitate as they enlighten. There's so much of our lives that we hastily bury, hoping all that restless mayhem stays settled beneath us.

Clark, however, will not allow our conjured calm. Although there's a tender, assured turn to his lyric, he remains steadfastly focused on what trouble does to the light. His search for father is heartrending. Consider "Those That Flew":

> Before the house I believe is my father's
> I stand, a rust-flecked fence
>
> between me & the answer. A latch
> I can't lift. Rain comes & I say,
>
> *Is this how it's supposed to be?*
> Soaked, unable to shield myself
>
> from what puddles at my feet.
> I don't carry his name the way
>
> I have his silhouette. Thunder sends birds
> scattering & I count the seconds

between each clap to gauge how fast
    the storm will come, though clearly,

it's here. From my mother
    I learned my name. I know

their song, but not what I should call
    those birds that flew.

You may think you've wandered this narrative landscape before. But you haven't. Not in this way.

And finally, the winner of this year's Miller Williams Poetry Prize—Alison Thumel's *Architect*.

I can't describe this book. I fill up every time I try. There's very little language huge enough to illustrate the depth of the poet's grief, her stark and tender transforming of it, her clenched containment of it as it pulses and bellows, straining to escape its borders.

There are so, so many ways to speak loss, but I've never experienced such structured tenderness, the building and rebuilding of what crafted the hollow. Alongside poems about Frank Lloyd Wright's creations, those glorious and lasting bodies, Thumel searches relentlessly for a lasting body her brother John might inhabit.

She has written often of John's death, and anyone who's barely lived through that grim upheaval will instantly recognize that anguished search for anything other than its bone-numbing torment.

Thumel builds and builds and loses and loses. And begins to build again.

Here I mark the spot where desolation
ended and began. Yet why mark this spot
if marking only remakes a misshapen
memory of the wound? The mark is dotted
like a line to form a charred and ugly
scar I run my fingers over, this path
I trace. Ended and began. Ended—see
I can mark the bounds of it. Nothing past

this wall I build, each brick a stitch I slip,
a slit I suture. Nothing—like trying
to see into a dark room before I dip
my hand far into that place. No small thing—
no stone, no wood, no work made of absence—
could mark you back into a present tense.

There are no words for what these words do.
And that's what it means to love poetry.

PATRICIA SMITH

ACKNOWLEDGMENTS

Thank you to Patricia Smith, David Scott Cunningham, and the University of Arkansas Press for believing in these words enough to help me share them with you. Thank you to Janet Foxman for your thorough edits and helpful questions.

Thank you to my cohort at the Callaloo Creative Writing Workshop, and our workshop leaders Vievee Francis and Gregory Pardlo.

Thank you to my colleagues at Rutgers University–Newark— Nadia, Colin, and Amy; and our teachers: A. Van Jordan, Rigoberto González, Brenda Shaughnessy, Kamilah Aisha Moon, and Christina Olivares.

Thank you to Mitchell L. H. Douglas, Kelly Norman Ellis, Ellen Hagan, and Dan Bernitt for pointing me down this path all those years ago.

Thank you to Emma Aprile for the thoughtful feedback that helped this manuscript finally click into place.

A special thanks to A. H. Jerriod Avant, Desiree Bailey, Nabila Lovelace, Chris Mattingly, Jayson P. Smith, Paul Tran, and Devon Walker-Figueroa—who read many versions of this manuscript along the way, whose careful attention and relentless encouragement were essential to the completion of this book, and for whose friendship I am forever grateful.

Thank you to my mother, who did not live long enough to read this book. Even when I didn't know it, it was her to whom I was writing all along.

Thank you to the journals and other outlets where some of these poems previously appeared, sometimes in different versions: *Callaloo, The Common, Day One, Foundry, Horsethief, Iowa Review, The Offing, Poem-a-Day, Poetry, Poetry Northwest, Prelude, Scalawag, Southern Review, The Spectacle, Vinyl, Washington Square Review, West Branch,* and *wildness.*

"Dear Darkness" appeared in the anthology *Soul Sister Revue: A Poetry Compilation*. "One Year Sober," "State of Denial," and "Southern Drawl" appeared in *Once a City Said: A Louisville Poets Anthology*. Some of these poems originally appeared in the chapbook *Some Blues I Know by Name*, published by alla testa press in 2017.

THE TROUBLE WITH LIGHT

MEMORY, FLOODING BACK

The river's rise out of itself began
in the west, the lowest part

of the city. The first breach:
subtle, just a thin film

of water over the land, like a hand
coaxing a child to sleep. Within hours,

it reached our home. The water
seeped through a window & I felt

so confused. How like a child,
to think the house has started to cry.

A PARTIAL LIST OF EFFECTS

Before me the heat rises off the blacktop.
      Before me, there was a man & a man
    & a man, which is to say violence

      endlessly revises. This lineage
I try to reject left me with a partial face:
      one eye black & the other welling

    though its tears won't fall. Black feathers
      in the street, caked in blood. Bouquet of dead
flowers I don't want to catch. Somewhere is a car

      & a driver ignorant of the harm he's done.
Have you ever dressed for school & slid
      your foot into a shoe to find a mouse

had crawled inside to die? *If there's one,*
      there's many & who knows better
    than exterminators the logic

      of infestation? What scratched in the walls
disappeared the scraps I wouldn't eat. Going hungry
      was a silent protest, a power that felt

    less like power than its shadow. Lack
turns the body into its own enemy:
      in the creases around my cracked smile,

            salt starts to show.

HOW DOES IT FEEL?

Outside, a blizzard reduced the skyline to suggestion. Snowed in,
I snuck peeks at my stepfather's mute television. Through the grain

I could see what looked like a hand caress what might have been
a thigh, until the image went out of focus. A month later,

I turned ten. Pressed against the television, I begged the camera,
lower. At the climax D'Angelo sang, *Let me take off your clothes & I'll*

but when his words wouldn't go further, I wanted
to know what his mind had fixed on, so that from within

surged something more than words: music, a moan, something
forced free. I'd seen what older boys on the bus claimed

they'd done. Through our thin walls I'd heard my mother's moans
& screams, his skin against hers, like a boot crunches through snow.

The night I entered their room & saw why
the bed sagged when I sat on its edge, what I had to say

I forgot. What those boys scrawled on the seats sometimes smeared
before it dried. When the screen filled with snow, my stepfather

                    smacked the set to bring the image back.

NEVER JUST ONE

One boy we called *filthy*
when he scratched his scalp.
Welfare kid, we teased, a hint
of white on his shoulder.
Lice, I feared you less
than the insults we hurled
at your suspected hosts.
When my mother found you
in my hair, I begged to go
to school, so she made me
swear I wouldn't tell,
& I tried, but when another kid
didn't board the bus that day
& whispers began to spread
suddenly I blurted out,
So what, I've got them too—
perhaps I couldn't pretend
I hadn't seen you writhe
in my mother's palm, like
how now I can't think of you
without remembering I too
have been forced from a place
I assumed would always be home:
sick of the man who'd rather
blow rent money on a high,
our mother hauled garbage bags
full of clothes out to the cab,
promising my brother & I we'd stay
in the shelter only two weeks.

I too have worried if I could keep
hidden, if I could keep anyone
from learning where we lived.
O head lice, O shame
whispered between two hands,
my scalp itches when I imagine
you, unnoticed as you spread
from shirt to shirt, from house
to house, nesting in a child's hair
until someone combs through his roots.

I LEARNED MY NAME WAS NOT MY NAME

He threw it from within the room
we never used unless company came. The radio
shattered in the kitchen, split my mother's scalp
until it bled. My stepfather called me
every name except my own. His backhand fed me
silence. A gag of knuckles. When I tried to fight
it wasn't enough. I can't remember if my brother
hid. The neighbors must've heard, must've
groaned, *Not again*. He stood over me & said,
Why stick up for her? She hasn't even told you
who your daddy really is. I was seven. The blood had set
in my mother's nightgown. She tried to blot
the stains. When I learned my name was
not my name, I became nobody's ghost. I grew inside
out. I curled my lips between my teeth & bit down
to not scream. He said, *I'll give you something*
to scream about—

Most nights I keep the radio on.
I feel something hover above me as I sleep.
My mother still says blood can be treated
with ice water, that a ghost is someone nobody believes
you've seen. When company came, he called
himself *father*, though that may have been a dream,
the last image before I woke. Over the music,
a muffled voice bleeds through the wall.
I sip from the glass on my desk. I press
against the cold, to hear.

SOME CALL IT ARTIFICIAL

Untangling the Christmas lights,
our mother teaches us curse words

no playground could. From under
a box marked *summer* I pull the tree

from the closet. We're careless
handlers so its branches are bent.

We aren't the kind to waste time
in some parking lot picking out

a live one: we have no car to carry it,
& besides, we hate those real trees

dropping needles on the floor.
Sweeping, watering, the necessary care

to keep something alive? No time.
Here's something we can store

year-round, something to break down
& stuff inside a box that will one day

be mostly tape. At least we have this:
one thing we take apart together.

When we can't count on gifts beneath
the tree, we count on the tree,

the lights that eventually flicker on.

DEAR DARKNESS

Forgive me & all
my missed

calls. We live
in what old

folks call trying
times, I mean

it's Monday,
it's that season

of the year the sun
sinks sooner

than I like.
I love most

about sunset
how it suggests

distance, a further
place where the

world curves
beyond what I see.

Before I knew
what to call you

I knew you. Dear
darkness, are we

headed someplace
new, someplace

not already in
our bones?

My folk swear
you're just

a phase, a spell,
some sort of down-

hearted song. Dear
darkness, is that you

at the piano,
you who troubles

the keys? Is
another word

for sorrow
consistency?

How we water
from our eyes

& call it anything
but persistence

beats me. I love
most the waiting

rooms, their still
dying flowers.

IN THE HOMETOWN I'VE TRIED TO LOVE

Perhaps the problem with this town
is that I think there's a problem with this town,
& not with how I care for my scars

no better than the body that bears them.
How I have lived for late nights, downing shots
like pennies tossed into a fountain, a devotion

practiced in dim rooms where, like billiard balls
sunk into side pockets, drunk men fall to their knees.
In his backyard my neighbor's digging a hole again

& though I know it's dramatic to say
it resembles a grave, what else would you call it
when your own thoughts drown you out? If it

takes two to be alone, I don't know which I'd rather be:
the one who stayed, or the one who walked away.

RERUN

What's on television is a rerun / You've seen every episode /
You know when the new ones air / Your homework is hard
to finish, sandwiched between your brother & two other boys
on a leather couch / Each bead of sweat slipping past the waist-
band of your shorts / Still in school clothes, you're not sure
when you'll be home / When your stepfather picked you
up from the bus stop, you erred on the side of silence /
The woman in the front seat wasn't your mother
but you'd seen her before /

                                The shows you watch are situational /
The cast always returns / From offstage you hear a coughing fit,
sharp inhales that let you know you'll be here awhile / Focus
on your lines / Spell *pipe* / Spell *hunger* / Spell *pawn*, not *lawn* /
Smell smoke as it wafts beneath the door / You call that handwriting? /
That's not how it should look / Your eraser gnawed off / Your step-
father, in the bedroom, doing whatever he does in rooms where
you aren't allowed / Look at the graphite smears where the words
should be / Hope the paper doesn't tear / The audience laughs
when they're told

HOW EASILY THEY SLAP

Tell them no one did this. Don't say, *I don't know my real father*. Don't
say you have a tongue you can't decipher. Don't believe in blank lips,
pill bottles, the pull

of pathology. How easily they slap
a label on a mouth. Don't explain how much you fear

the lurch of a passing train, the sound of boxcars
rattling back to life. Tell them he's been

good to you. Tell them if they lay a finger
on your Adam's apple they'll understand. If they ask *why*,
don't say you're a walking root.

WHOLE LIFE

You drove hearses most your life, yet before you died
  you said you'd never seen a corpse. *Wasn't my job
    to look*, was how you left it, as you unraveled

      the seams on your chair. You never felt a need
to explain how your breakfast came to be
  half a pack of Kools & a cold glass of water,
             or how you found yourself

      in that line of work. I suspected you the sort of man
who tolerated the dead more than the living, judging
  by the way you kept all our conversations short: a quick

      wave of your hand meant our time was coming
to an end. Some weekends now I post up near the far end
  of my favorite bar, within earshot of the older guys

      who regale each other with war stories. No two tellings
are ever the same, but rather than privilege the facts
  over the feelings, I nod, & when they go quiet

      I see you, silently driving that hearse,
the manicured body of someone else's loved one
  only a few feet behind your head, like a thought on the tip

      of your tongue, like a word you'd never again recall.

STATE OF DENIAL

As though there were no North Star.
As though beneath the white oak one might find shade
    & not find oneself

dreaded from the branches.

In a front yard, on cinder blocks,
the scrapped hull of what'll get fixed
one day, one day . . .

as though the air won't keep its promise, won't turn steel
to flaking rust. As though light doesn't still fall
from something dead long ago.

There are some who like to think
this state was never divided,

as though here we don't have brothers
    with eyes & barrels aimed,

as though distance isn't the measure of everything
between us

           & what we can't see,

as though dread isn't what sways the trees,
as though one could turn away from that,

as though this wasn't the enslaved side of the river.

WHAT'S LEFT

A therapist said my father's absence
    left inside me an impulse to hit,

like the cave paintings of a people
    who have abandoned their home.

Tell me what anyone expects to learn
    from what others leave behind.

If you better understand a boy's rage
    after he shows you the plaster wall

he put his fist through, know I hid
    those holes beneath a poster

of Jimi Hendrix kneeling over a guitar
    he set on fire. Today I wake up

with the imprint of headphones in my hair
    from trying to mask the sound

of my mother absorbing the blows
    of a man I couldn't defend her from.

A closer look at her neck reveals
    the handprint she's concealed.

In her throat, a harsh whisper.
    I can still hear what she's endured.

WORDS OF WARNING

Before a screw in the rail broke the skin
on my hand as I told my brother not to open
the door for anyone. I mean before I left

him there alone. Before I told my friend's
mother *I can't explain why I need
to leave* & she said *be there soon.*

Before I crammed my backpack full
with, yes, a change of clothes but also
pens & paper & books for school

while in the living room my brother turned
the TV's volume low. Before he sank
back into the couch & before he crawled

from beneath the bed. Before I yelled
Lord I can't take this or whispered *How
long you think we should wait until we*

move again. Before that. Before the thud
of footsteps down the stairs receded,
& even before we could hear nothing

but our own held breath, our hearts
beating like impatient fists against doors
as we wondered if the quiet meant

he was gone. Before I began to wonder
if a cough or the way my brother winces
as he tongues a cut in his mouth might

give us away, give a man an idea
of where to aim a gun as he raps his fist
against the window, as his shadow stains

the drapes. Before my brother muted
the television when I said *I can't explain*
you just have to hide & urged him

under the bed. It was before I peeked
through the blinds thinking I'd see who
knocked on the neighbor's door, & locked

eyes with a man in a black hat who waved
the pistol in his hand. Before we died
laughing at a cartoon hunter foiled again

by a rabbit. Before we heard the dead-
bolt slide into place. Before our mother
said to us *Don't answer the door*

for anyone & left with a woman
who begged for help on our porch.
Before that knock on the door. Before

we were sure to close every set of blinds
to keep the house cool. Before the news
said it'd be a hot one today. Before drops

of blood appeared in the peaches
my brother ate straight from the can,
its serrated edge snagging the inside

of his lip when he tipped it back to down
the juice. For him, that was the best part.
Before he went to the fridge, he said

he was in the mood for something sweet.

FIXING TO DIE

how could you
ever stop

the whine of a dog
wanting free of its leash

≈

what unnerves you:
the horn of
a southbound

train   the backfire
of a passing car
a heavy door swung

shut   a man's laugh
through the wall
the scrape

of a chair
across the floor
also silence

a cat's eyes
trained on something
you can't see

≈

so often you
go to town
on a handle

of whiskey
lips glued
until tore up

until a stream
of piss
in the alley

a dried trail
of vomit on
your chin

≈

how dare you
trace with your feet

the edge
of any bridge

≈

stench of sour milk
of night sweats
& soaked sheets

hanging from
the door
a limp

towel looks
in the dark
like an answer

to a question
you've been
wanting to ask

THOSE THAT FLEW

Before the house I believe is my father's
   I stand, a rust-flecked fence

between me & the answer. A latch
   I can't lift. Rain comes & I say,

Is this how it's supposed to be?
   Soaked, unable to shield myself

from what puddles at my feet.
   I don't carry his name the way

I have his silhouette. Thunder sends birds
   scattering & I count the seconds

between each clap to gauge how fast
   the storm will come, though clearly,

it's here. From my mother
   I learned my name. I know

their song, but not what I should call
   those birds that flew.

THIS WATERFALL COULD NEVER STILL

Sprawled out in a stranger's yard
you've numbed yourself again.
      Your forearms prove how

dull a blade can be. As night coils around us
    like smoke from a snuffed cigarette,
headlights pass, white as pills

      on a porcelain sink. Brother, worry
has worn our mother's voice. We
    wait beside you, knowing it's best

    not to count how long it's been.
Each breath from your lungs
      is a flame she cups to keep lit

    & all her sentences start: *I need*—
      Your eyes roll back
& a screen door slams,

      a dog circles its crate,
a lamp switches off in one house,
      then another.

It's not exactly sadness I feel
when I hear the wind disturb
    someone's chimes, the backfire

of an old Ford. Like you I have
nights I can't remember. A history of
hardly caring for my body, of letting

whoever drink their share of me,
thinking it could cure
my fear of dirt, how soon

it'll kiss me with an open mouth.
I don't want to be alone, you say,
as the mosquitoes get their fill.

AND JUST LIKE THAT RIVER, I'VE BEEN RUNNING

It's hard to call you
a body, that word
for what's still,

knowing you
lap at my soles,
dare me waist-deep

into a murk the shade
of my skin. Tell me:
if not knowing how

to swim I still wade
into deeper waters
am I brave or do I want

it all to end? I used to
think how the wind
made its way around

my body meant a kind
of agency. I used to think
you were there to keep me

from a different state.
On the bank, my blood
courses through me

so hard, my heart
tosses like a buoy
in a coal freighter's wake.

Braided in the trees, balloons
& caution tape, a pair
of shoes once owned by

a boy once someone's friend,
someone's blood, a boy
a stray bullet made a stream.

THE MEN, AS I REMEMBER THEM

1.

Mostly, fleeting.

Not entirely filled with anger,
but yes, anger, suppressed
until it wasn't. I remember them best

by what they kept between their legs:
pistols, brown-bagged pints of liquor . . .
Tenderness:

a power none could wield
without harm.
Given these models,

I would rather have had none.
I'm tired all the time now.
Most nights, I'm up
later than I'd like, but there's no better
bar than home.
I wouldn't say I'm intent

on ending it, this life:
some part of me thinks it's possible
to shed those memories.

2.

Knowing it's impossible
to shed those memories,
    what better home than a bar?

            Better?
                    I want to be
        but I'm tired all the time now. Most nights,

                        I'd rather have one more
                                & try to remember
                    when I was without harm.

                            Given these models,
            I would rather have a power
                none could wield

                            between their legs.
                    No pistols. No brown liquor.
                    A tenderness.

            Remember me best
                        by what was fleeting.
                Not entirely anger,

                            but, yes, anger.

LAST NIGHT IN LOUISVILLE

I didn't wake this morning
because I never slept. For what felt
   like the final time I crawled

   through the window of an old life.
      All night I laughed with a woman
   who snuffed fires with her palm.

   Leaving the bar, she slipped a faded photo
   in my pocket. In it, I was clean-
shaven, wide-eyed, not like now. Now,

      my mind's a flickering streetlight,
a pint glass stained with the last drops
   of what made my stomach clench. Now,

   the microphone's off. I've lost my keys,
      a book & a candle I was given.
   The book: one I already owned

      but inscribed with a message for me.
   Raised to think I'd leave someday, here
   I sit, at the gate, too drunk to see

      the wheels touch down, the smoke
   trailing behind. An airport toilet
      the last thing I hugged.

   Tossing my keys in a drawer,
      a bartender waits for me to call.

NOW YOU SEE IT

Running away is an urge I've always had
faith in. If I could afford a therapist
I bet they'd say it's perfectly fine

to feel this way, even if some see me
as plain crazy. I turned twenty-six

the way a man turns onto a street
where he once lived, his casual stroll
raising suspicion. Call me crazy

but who's that peeking out their blinds
as I pass their house? I've left whole

boxes of my belongings stacked inside
a room I couldn't be bothered to clean,
so quickly I needed to leave, to escape

the neighbor at my door, swinging
a bat as he swore the Black folk living

on his street, by sunset, would be dead.
Of course he called it his. He called himself
keeping watch in his off-kilter rocking

chair, surrounded by a cemetery
of beer cans, crushed & chucked all over

his yard. His piss-drunk laugh
like a kettle's whistle. I'd been warned
about men like this, about having to share

a fence with them. I've long since moved
but won't even go outside to mow. Weeds

have taken over my lawn, but the news says
when folks ignore the warning signs
they're likely to die of exposure these days.

THE SOUTH GOT SOMETHING TO SAY

Not an ounce of your body's blood
is yours alone, yet you dare

carry it across state lines,
knowing what happens to anyone caught

with that kind of contraband.
You might think you have no accent,

                        but open your mouth
& I'm all they hear. Not a word you say
belongs to you.

                    A Cadillac's trunk,
an empty pantry, dumpster, grave:

what makes the shape of your mouth
any different?

WHATEVER VEHICLE GETS YOU THROUGH

So I've been curious about this bird
I see when I take the train to class.

One might confuse it for a crane,
confuse it for a sign. Sometimes
        a flock appears beside the tracks,

& sometimes I spot only one, alone
        in a peat green marsh, & goddamn

if I'm not relieved by the sight
        of a marsh amid all this glass & rust.
As a child I dreamt up cities,

        I dreamt up maps & drew them inside
notebooks & folders, on any scrap

        of paper I could find. I obsessed over
streets & highways above all else.
        On the interstate, I would fix my eyes

on everything that passed below:
        this neighborhood I'd never been to,

that neighborhood no longer home.
        By age twelve, we'd moved so often
I thought motion was my natural state.

Stillness? A trap. It was the worst
in church: the endless sermons

I could never follow, the stiff pews,
the summers we waved those futile fans.
Others leapt out of their seats & fell

to their knees, mouths suddenly full
of strange tongues. Told by the elders

they'd caught the spirit, I saw proof
the church needed a new AC.
Still today no one would claim me

as a man with faith in much,
though sometimes in that dark

moment before the train emerges
from the tunnel, I look forward
to that marsh, to those birds

I now expect to see, that view of the city
I'm speeding away from, the light.

ONE FIRE, QUENCHED WITH ANOTHER

1.
Pained as he was when he gazed
upon his father's face, he held his gaze.

2.
Toward what he'd never known,
he walked, somehow
both arrogant & begging.

The purple of his father's robes, like a bruise.

3.
A river, over time, forges
a way through stone.

Absence bore through him,
left a valley where his voice
echoed off the canyon walls.

4.
His mind had narrowed until all it held
was an idea of father, until so fixed on the idea
his mind seemed under siege. Inside him hummed
a longing, one he felt compelled to fix, so named it *flaw*.

5.
What the boy wanted:
to finally know his father's face.
Evidence, at last, of his origin.

6.

Felt within, a longing.
Felt & therefore knew
a weakness he wanted to master.

7.

A desire to know, & a belief
he deserved to,

these were the human parts of him.

8.

Fiery, Dawnsteed, Scorcher, Blaze—

the horses the father owned,

the horses the father, knowing he would fail, let his son steer—

9.

is this devotion?

10.

To master, control, rein in;
hoping this might prove him
a man, perhaps, a god.

11.

There are gaps knowing cannot fill.

12.

What boy has not dreamt himself a noble son,
has not prematurely thought himself a man?

13.

He lost control of the reins
& the horses did what one expects
from animals whose lives had always been
tightly squeezed between two fists:

14.

breaking from the path they'd always known,

15.

they galloped nearer to that world from which they'd been kept,

16.

not out of malice but a kind of sympathy

17.

for the world the father feared the horses would harm.

18.

Finding himself at the mercy of what he'd sought—

19.

gone too far to turn back, gone far beyond his father now
with further still to go, ignorant of the names

of the horses behind whom he now trailed like the tail
of a comet hurtling toward earth, as in all directions
he sees the destruction he'd caused:

the flames licking trees at their roots, licking
dry the ocean's mouth, licking the faces
of each living thing until they'd turned to ash,

until the world without grew hotter than the world within,
until a dizzying heat rose from the soil, until in his feet

20.
the boy could feel the world ablaze—

21.
free me from these reins
he cried perhaps to god,
perhaps to father,

22.
the difference indecipherable, more or less insignificant

23.
for even though he'd met him, the boy still knew himself

24.
fatherless, godless, no less abandoned than he'd been.

25.

The world to which, for better or worse, he once belonged, now gone,

26.

he belonged nowhere.

27.

To save what could be saved, to salvage what had not been lost,
to punish his failure to master what no other ever had: the boy

28.

was struck dead & buried

29.

beside a river, which began again to flow toward the distant mouth

30.

out of which it would finally empty.

SOUTHERN DRAWL

Here is where the bloodhounds tried to dig up
what's rested in the dirt. Before dawn, I searched
for what haunts me & found I'm a man after my own
shadow. Who could stand to hear a tongue forged
into shape? Someone says *mastery*

                        & I hear *misery*.
Cracked lips, I wish you a wetting. I love nothing
more than the damp field behind my teeth, where a stable-
boy turns loose the wild horse none could break.

INDEPENDENCE DAY

Come morning,

   let the ants have what traces

of wine drip on the sill.

      Tonight the reds, whites,

   & blues bloom

      above rooftops, disrupting

   the dark.

   Given history,

         it's hard to enjoy

   such spectacle.

            I thought I was here alone

but behind me, smiling,

      you watch me drink.

   You think *love* is the best

         word to describe how clean

   I lick my palm.

YOU HAVE TO GO AWAY TO COME BACK

As a boy I was a rowdy beast.
I refused leashes, cages,

sought out the cleanest palm
from which to feed. I received

counsel from a flashy pastor
who worshipped a slumlord God,

who said not to sublet myself
as from the collection plate

he slyly pocketed bills. As if I
were the only one who would fall

for lovers who could strip me
with just a whisper of my name.

I fulfilled their simplest wishes
yet come morning, like a dove

my heart returned, failing to find
dry land. For years I've wandered

in this bare-assed stupor,
two of each kind of longing in tow.

BAXTER, BETWEEN HIGHLAND AND PAYNE

No longer entranced by the neon signs on this avenue, the bars
whose names once meant the same to him: release, relief—
Relief, perhaps, from the crooked

contours of a body distorted by desire. Night after night,
overheard barstool confessions convinced him
we must all be accidents. Like anyone lost,
he can't recall if he was exiled

or if he escaped. What a stranger his own body
has become. He daydreams now about other men
he could have been. His hands, tired from grasping
for anyone who could, he hoped, bear him—

but who could bear him?
In whoever undressed him, he saw
a spotless mirror. Someone who could help him mask
his shattered teeth, his blackened eyes.

(I AM) MY FATHER'S SON

you grew into
a void.
unbelievably
articulate.
i knew you'd never hold me
responsible.

i too was taught to leave.
trace the contours of my face.
pay attention: a solitary heart is
no heart at all

a name i'd never heard,
i tiptoed around its edges.
blank, unable to
remember this face.
& i wanted to hold you

but you're only a ghost.
an outline
in the mirror. i waited.
one hand open. still, you had
to turn around.

AFTER THE CREST

One of the spared, I'm left
       to wonder, *Why me.*

    I fashion a raft from remnants
of the life I've lost
      & drift

      through the waterlogged rooms. Below
the water's indifferent face:
    cars, wardrobes, keepsakes, rocking chairs,
     splintered—

    A catfish swims
      through a shattered window.

On the roof of their home, two girls
     orphaned by the flood.

      I don't know what matters now.

    Huddled in the jacket my drowned
father always wore, I lower
     my cupped hand
       into the water,

    which seeps through my fingers
       as I bring it to my lips.

DOING THE WORK

One hand holding the tongue
as the other grips the cloth,

I polish my boots, as if
ruin could be shined away.

To no one, I say, *These will dull
like anything relied on daily.*

The trouble with light
is its insistence:

the curtain's failure to block it out
may be a flaw, but not one

it can help. Last night again
I dreamt myself

in a patch of wild-
berries, bending to have

a mouthful, unworried
if they were safe to taste. Disaster,

galloping down the fence line,
stirring up dust with its storm of hooves,

hadn't yet disappeared. Laughing,
I felt the juice trickle down my chin

& I rose, saying, *Bitter, so bitter.*

THERE'S NO IGNORING IT NOW

For days, doubt struck as does lightning
across the span of night. Illuminated that way,

how did we cross the river? One stone,
then another. The silence between us a keyhole

through which I peeked & found you teasing
off your robe. Love? If it exists,

it's the uncertainty one feels before a thunderclap,
after the sky's gone dark again. O prick

of hope—I am too numb. The stir of weaker
creatures seeking safety: from afar, one could

call it beautiful. Even if you can't,
I recall those mornings, the dappled light

spat across my cheeks. When you disrobed
before the window, whose eyes did you hope to catch:

mine, or your own, reflected in the glass?
Before the owl swoops in & snatches it up,

before it's dead, when the lone mouse hesitates,
then steps into the clearing, is that faith,

or foolishness?

NO ANGEL

Would it matter if he was?

Chickens peck his feathers loose.

Like the water keeps up its quiet lapping,

strange eyes visit at night, curious

if he sleeps. When awake, his eyes are star-

latched, his fingers lace the cage's wire.

The neighbors skip their nightly gossip.

The neighbors whisper, *It must end soon.*

Each day, more feathers line the cage floor.

When the time comes, bury him close

to the sea. Where each grain of sand

can be his. Where you can see the wind

force seagulls back to shore.

GOLDEN HOUR

the first hour after the occurrence of a traumatic injury

No mirror filled with an overwhelming glare.
No backsliding from the pinnacle of promise, or was it
purpose? No discovery that love has fallen, toothlike,

from my mouth as I slept. No life sorted into piles: *ruined,
not ruined yet.* Nothing that amounts to only regret.
Not another spent match, its smoke curled upward

as if charmed. No doorless hallway where you watch me
stumble through the dance called Obligation.
Let's not pretend.
                    Don't ask me to sing a song
whose lyrics have fogged over in my mind.

Come spring, from the shards of a desire I once
choked down, I'll fashion a flowerpot. Not an urn.

There's no home to which, if I wanted to, I could return.

ONE YEAR SOBER

Can't say I miss that

        beach where on every walk I burned

                my feet

that time the swarm

           of wasps took over

        the church

Each day was once

       a bitterness I couldn't bear

             without a drink

was once a glass

      door smudged by everyone

          who ever left

I was a plastic cup

        rattled & filling with whatever

      others could spare

The future just a model

home I couldn't imagine

calling my own

If a cluttered desk

emptied by a sweeping hand

can be considered cleaned

I suppose it was

sometimes peaceful

how a drink could clear my mind

Now at night I count

the planes above & trace

the path that brought me

here

to this house

where restless in the dark

I stare at that familiar spot

on the wall: those newly laid bricks

in the shape of a door

IN THE HOMETOWN I'VE TRIED TO LOVE

Remember earlier, when I showed you
around town, how all my maps were mental,

my sense of direction based on landmarks
long gone? A kind of proof, you said, of how

so clearly I'm a small-town boy, pointing out
ghosts wherever I go. In bed with you,

calm as a city just after a storm—
your eyes, two wet leaves on a windshield,

my hand, still as a stalled car in the small
of your back—& still I can't get out of my mind

the spiderwebs spun in the corners of this room,
how this whole building's unstable.

Years from now it'll be condemned, reduced
to rubble, & they'll build over it, or not,

just leave it forever an empty lot, one more
memorial dedicated to neglect. By now, you know

how most of my stories end: someone walks out
on the porch, wonders which will be the storm

that splinters the oak, that levels the walls.

WHAT I SEE WHEN I STARE LONG ENOUGH INTO NOTHING

A screen door easing shut:
the only way I can describe
this creaking in my knees.
It's when I'm alone that this pain
is easy to hear. I haven't been
a child in years yet here I go,
discussing the past again.
I've been told what happened to me
doesn't define me, matters less
than the narrative I tell. At night
I rub coconut oil into my skin,
over the scar on my arm
in the shape of a garden
snake. I can tell it
disappoints you, how I can't recall
its origin, but trust me, it doesn't
matter now. Seeping through my fingers
the oil reminds me of rain,
how at first it gently settles
into soil. Unless there's a storm,
at which point picture a child,
ignoring what they've been told,
who finds a way to ruin
their shoes. And picture a mother,
relieved when finally her child
returns. Even if he leaves
the door ajar. Even if he leaves
footprints on the floor.

STILL I DREAM ABOUT BIRDS

Because I've almost killed myself

trying to leave a house I never

asked to enter. Because I've hoped

my hands would one day evolve

away. Because it's my mouth I've used most

to alter, receive. Seed, dead limbs:

what my mother's chewed to make

my eating easier. Because I've shrunk

to adapt. Because some days I swerve

to avoid slamming into a threat I can't see.

Because I am one of many

whose original names no one recalls,

brought here in the hold

& named *invasive*. Because to remain

still requires so much motion. Because

even my speech sounds like a song.

UNAUTHORIZED AUTOBIOGRAPHY

a cento

Down in the valley,
the illest villains
hotwire my heart.
They say I'm different,
super stupid,
everything in between
the bad & the beautiful,
the black saint & the sinner lady.
Ain't no tellin'
everything I am.
Time has told me
misery is a butterfly,
dirty blue gene,
common heat.
Bootsy, what's the name of this town?
Expressway to your skull.
Republic of rough & ready.
Call me
slum beautiful,
two-headed boy,
one chapter in the book
Everybody Knows This Is Nowhere.
Have you ever been
between two worlds,
looking for astronauts?
Someone's always singing
softly, as in a morning sunrise.
How strange, innocence,

grinning in your face.
                    I need a forest fire,
          blue & sentimental,
born of a broken man.
     Calling all demons:
               choose your weapon.
     Dance, or die.

OTHER, ENTIRELY

You think the morning brings a kind
light, a clarity, forgetting everything
night makes possible, how we learned

our way around each other. You say,
This is what distinguishes a home
from a place one has simply slept,

& I think you mean, having watched me
for many nights now undress & dress,
you know me. What about me

proves I am who you think?
Within a stranger must be a light
by which I can guide myself: I once clung

to such belief. Before the mirror now
I stand, still naked, until my reflection
feels apart from me, until it seems no different

than the tree in the window, stripped of leaves.
No, it's more like the leaves themselves:
scattered, even more subject to the wind.

HOME

the technical impossibilities of return don't make return impossible,
except in the ways that there isn't there anymore

—Fred Moten

at best a word

                          a want

I can barely mouth.

                          to go back—

how false it feels:

                          to firmly grip

those dangling threads,

                          & wrap myself in

                what I never had.

THEY BOLTED & BROUGHT HIM LOW

1.

Dragging beside them now the boy, his body

a purple unlike that shade reserved for royalty,

ankles tangled in the reins, no more able to free himself

than they can rid themselves of him,

the horses keep their stride, galloping

not toward anywhere, lacking guidance (unless *away from*

harm can be a kind of aim, then that);

≈

undirected,

not yet riderless, they gallop even harder

than when whipped, as if effort

had always been the answer.

2.

Not a question entered his mind at the reins,

where he'd felt secure, closest to that ideal

he aspired to: that of a boy able to go

where he pleases, so no longer a boy, but a man,

& so a cloudless sky

                            looked, then, like possibility.

From a lower vantage now, it seems as if his

is only one of many dilemmas along a dirt road

that leads . . . where? There are countless ways a boy is drawn

≈

toward risk: curiosity, apathy, a need to numb

a shame born out of belonging, in a sense,

nowhere; all easily confused from afar,

≈

as hard to discern as, between the rider & the horses,

who suffers more—

≈

                      as if knowing mattered.

As if knowing put either at ease. Like a cloud

of dust kicked up by hooves, now settling

on his cracked, bleeding skin, across the boy's face

something spread: a look of calm; of one,

perhaps, knowing his limits, that

human part of him: two hands, struggling to grasp the reins.

    Then two hands, letting go.

NOTES

"I Learned My Name Was Not My Name" is a line from the Robert Hayden poem "Names."

"And Just Like That River, I've Been Running" takes its title from the Sam Cooke song "A Change Is Gonna Come."

"Now You See It" borrows a rhetorical move from Jericho Brown's "Another Elegy," published in his collection *The New Testament*.

"The South Got Something to Say" takes its title from André 3000, who said these words in Outkast's acceptance speech at the 1995 Source Awards.

"One Fire, Quenched with Another" and "They Bolted & Brought Him Low" both take their titles from lines in David Raeburn's translation of Ovid's *Metamorphoses*.

"(I Am) My Father's Son" borrows a line from Antonio Machado's "Moral Proverbs and Folksongs," translated by Mary G. Berg and Dennis Maloney, as published in *The Ecco Anthology of International Poetry*.

"Golden Hour" is after Lucie Brock-Broido's poem "A Girl Ago" from her collection *Stay, Illusion*.

The title "What I See When I Stare Long Enough into Nothing" references a line from Ada Limón's poem "The Great Blue Heron of Dunbar Road," published in her collection *Bright Dead Things*.

"Unauthorized Autobiography" is a cento composed of song and album titles in my digital music library.